HOW TO DRAW™
MANGA
ACTION FIGURES

David Antram

BOOK 🪓 HOUSE

SALARIYA

Published in Great Britain in MMXII by
Book House, an imprint of
The Salariya Book Company Ltd
25 Marlborough Place, Brighton BN1 1UB

1 3 5 7 9 8 6 4 2

Please visit our website at **www.salariya.com** for **free** electronic versions of:
You Wouldn't Want to Be an Egyptian Mummy!
You Wouldn't Want to Be a Roman Gladiator!
Avoid Joining Shackleton's Polar Expedition!
Avoid Sailing on a 19th-Century Whaling Ship!

Author: **David Antram** was born in Brighton, England, in 1958. He studied at Eastbourne College of Art and then worked in advertising for fifteen years before becoming a full-time artist. He has illustrated many children's non-fiction books.

Editor: Victoria England

PB ISBN: 978-1-908177-21-6

A CIP catalogue record for this book is available from the British Library.

Printed and bound in China.
Printed on paper from sustainable sources.

WARNING: Fixatives should be used only under adult supervision.

Visit our websites to read interactive free web books, stay up to date with new releases, catch up with us on the Book House Blog, view our electronic catalogue and more!

www.book-house.co.uk
Information books
and graphic novels

www.scribobooks.com
Fiction books

www.scribblersbooks.com
Books for babies, toddlers and
pre-school children.

Follow us on Facebook and
Twitter by visiting
www.salariya.com

PAPER FROM
SUSTAINABLE
FORESTS

Contents

Making a start

Learning to draw is about looking and seeing. Keep practising and get to know your subject. Use a sketchbook to make quick sketches. Start by doodling and experimenting with shapes and patterns. There are many ways to draw; this book shows one method. Visit art galleries, look at artists' drawings, see how friends draw, but above all, find your own way.

Use simple shapes at first to try out different action poses.

Perspective

If you look at any object from different viewpoints, you will see that the part that is closest to you looks larger, and the part furthest away from you looks smaller. Drawing in perspective is a way of creating a feeling of space — of showing three dimensions on a flat surface.

V.P.

The vanishing point (V.P.) is the place in a perspective drawing where parallel lines appear to meet. The position of the vanishing point depends on the viewer's eye level. Sometimes an unusually high or low viewpoint can give your drawing added drama.

V.P.

Two-point perspective drawing

Two-point perspective uses two vanishing points: one for lines running along the length of the figure, and one on the opposite side for lines running across the width of the figure.

Low eye level
(view from below)

Normal eye level

High eye level
(view from above)

V.P. = vanishing point

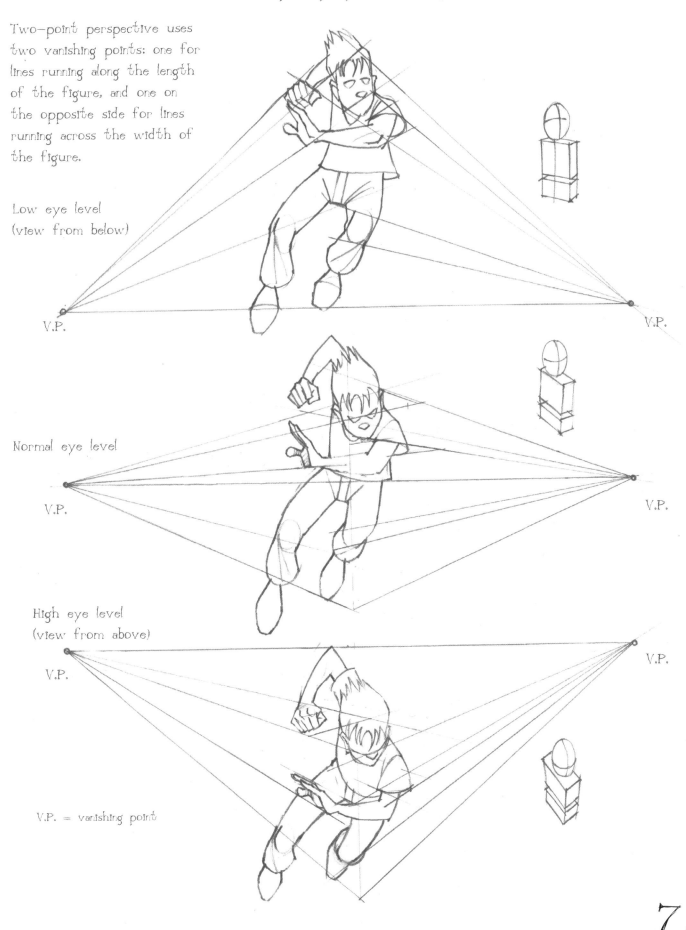

V.P.

V.P.

V.P.

V.P.

V.P.

V.P.

7

Drawing tools

Here are just a few of the many tools that you can use for drawing. Let your imagination go, and have fun experimenting with all the different marks you can make.

Pencil

Watercolour pencil

Charcoal pencil

Charcoal stick

Pastels

Finger painting

Black, grey and white pastel on grey sugar paper

Each grade of **pencil** makes a different mark, from fine, grey lines through to soft, black ones. Hard pencils are graded as H, 2H, 3H, 4H, 5H and 6H (the hardest). An HB pencil is ideal for general sketching. Soft pencils are graded from B, 2B, 3B, 4B, 5B to 6B (the softest and blackest).

Watercolour pencils come in many different colours and make a line similar to an HB pencil. But paint over your finished drawing with clean water, and the lines will soften and run.

It is less messy and easier to achieve a fine line with a **charcoal pencil** than a stick of charcoal. Create soft tones by smudging lines with your finger. **Ask an adult** to spray the drawing with fixative to prevent further smudging.

Pastels are brittle sticks of powdered colour. They blend and smudge easily and are ideal for quick sketches. Pastel drawings work well on textured, coloured paper. **Ask an adult** to spray your finished drawing with fixative.

Experiment with **finger painting**. Your fingerprints make exciting patterns and textures. Use your fingers to smudge soft pencil, charcoal and pastel lines.

Ballpoint pens are very useful for sketching and making notes. Make different tones by building up layers of shading.

A **mapping pen** has to be dipped into bottled ink to fill the nib. Different nib shapes make different marks. Try putting a diluted ink wash over parts of the finished drawing.

Draughtsmen's pens and specialist **art pens** can produce extremely fine lines and are ideal for creating surface texture. A variety of pen nibs are available which produce different widths of line.

Felt—tip pens are ideal for quick sketches. If the ink is not waterproof, try drawing on wet paper and see what happens.

Broad—nibbed **marker pens** make interesting lines and are good for large, bold sketches. Try using a black pen for the main sketch and a grey one to block in areas of shadow.

Paintbrushes are shaped differently to make different marks. Japanese brushes are soft and produce beautiful flowing lines. Large sable brushes are good for painting a wash over a line drawing. Fine brushes are good for drawing delicate lines.

9

Materials

Try using different types of drawing papers and materials. Experiment with charcoal, wax crayons and pastels. All pens, from felt-tips to ballpoints, will make interesting marks. Try drawing with pen and ink on wet paper.

Silhouette is a style of drawing which mainly uses solid black shapes.

Ink silhouette

Felt-tips come in a range of line widths. The wider pens are good for filling in large areas of flat tone.

Lines drawn in **ink** cannot be erased, so keep your ink drawings sketchy and less rigid. Don't worry about mistakes, as these can be lost in the drawing as it develops.

It can be tricky adding light and shade to a drawing with a pen. Use a solid layer of ink for the very darkest areas and cross-hatching (straight lines criss-crossing each other) for ordinary dark tones. Hatching (straight lines running parallel to each other) can be used for midtones.

Cross-hatching

Hatching

Pencil drawings can include a vast amount of detail and tone. Try experimenting with the different grades of pencil to get a range of light and shade effects in your drawing.

Remember, the best equipment and materials will not necessarily make the best drawing — only practice will!

Action poses

Motion and balance are important aspects to consider in your drawing. Use basic construction lines to create a variety of poses. Then build the drawing up from there.

Exaggerate the curve of the centre line to give movement and action to your figure.

Add shading to any areas where light would not reach.

Study real people to see how their bodies move.

Pay particular attention to the curve and direction of the spine and hips.

Use construction lines to make sure the balance of the fighting figures is accurate.

Use circle and oval shapes to position the joints.

Keep the drawing quite light and sketchy at first, until you are confident that the proportions are right.

13

Adding movement

The style and position of the movement lines that you draw can create many different types of fighting movement.

Start by sketching these simple shapes.

Head

Body

Draw an oval for the head and body and smaller ovals for the hands.

Sketch in the arms using straight lines. Add dots to indicate the joints.

Using your construction lines as a guide, sketch simple tube shapes for the arms.

Sketch in the positions of the facial features and hair.

Complete the facial features.

Add circles for the joints.

Add shading and tone to create muscle definition.

14

By changing the position and style of the movement lines, you can change the action of the figure.

Curved, sweeping lines create the effect of an arc-shaped punch.

Straight lines drawn in one direction give the impression of strong impact.

Faded movement lines create the effect that the hand is moving very fast.

15

Jumping Fighter

This character is launching himself off the ground and swinging a punch at the same time.

Start by sketching simple shapes for the figure.

Head

Body

Hips

Indicate the joints with dots.

Draw two lines to indicate the position and angle of the shoulders and hips. Draw a line for the spine.

Sketch in the positions of the facial features.

Using the construction lines as a guide, start drawing in the main shapes of the body.

Draw in tube shapes for the legs; note how the legs appear shorter as they angle towards or away from the viewer.

Add ovals for the feet.

Add the outline of
the clothing.

Draw in the fingers in a
clenched fist shape.

Add the curved
structure of the
upper body and
indicate the position
of the belt.

Add more detail
to the face and
sketch in the hair.

Add lines to
indicate movement.

Complete the
facial features.

Shade the bottom
half of the leg.

Draw in the details
of the clothing.

Complete the drawing
of the boots.

Remember to remove any
unwanted construction lines.

Shade any areas
where light would
not reach.

17

Martial arts

Manga figures are often shown in action, performing martial arts moves.

Start by sketching these simple shapes for the figure.

Sketch an oval for the head.

Add an overlapping oval for the body and another for the hips.

Draw the limbs with straight lines.

Indicate the joints with dots.

Add circles for the joints.

Draw oval shapes to position the feet.

Sketch in the positions of the hands using curved shapes.

Sketch in the positions of the headband and nose.

Using your construction lines as a guide, sketch simple tube shapes for the arms and legs.

Draw in the shape of the fingers.

Manga characters generally have very stylised hair. Think about the situation and make the hair fit the scene.

Draw in the shape of the clothes, making sure that they go around the body and flare out at the ends of the limbs.

Add spiky hair and start to finish the face.

Draw the toes on the feet.

Add creases to the cloth.

Complete the facial features.

Add shading and tone to the clothes.

Complete the feet and ankles.

Remove any unwanted construction lines.

Mecha giant robot

This humanoid robot is ready to do battle!

Draw two lines to indicate the position and angle of the shoulders and hips. Draw in a line for the spine.

Head

Draw different-sized ovals for the head, body and hips.

Body

Draw simple lines for the limbs, adding dots at the joints.

Hips

Sketch in oval shapes for the hands.

Sketch in the shape of the arms and legs, adding circles for both elbows and knees.

Start sketching in the robot's mechanical fingers.

Draw rounded shapes for the feet.

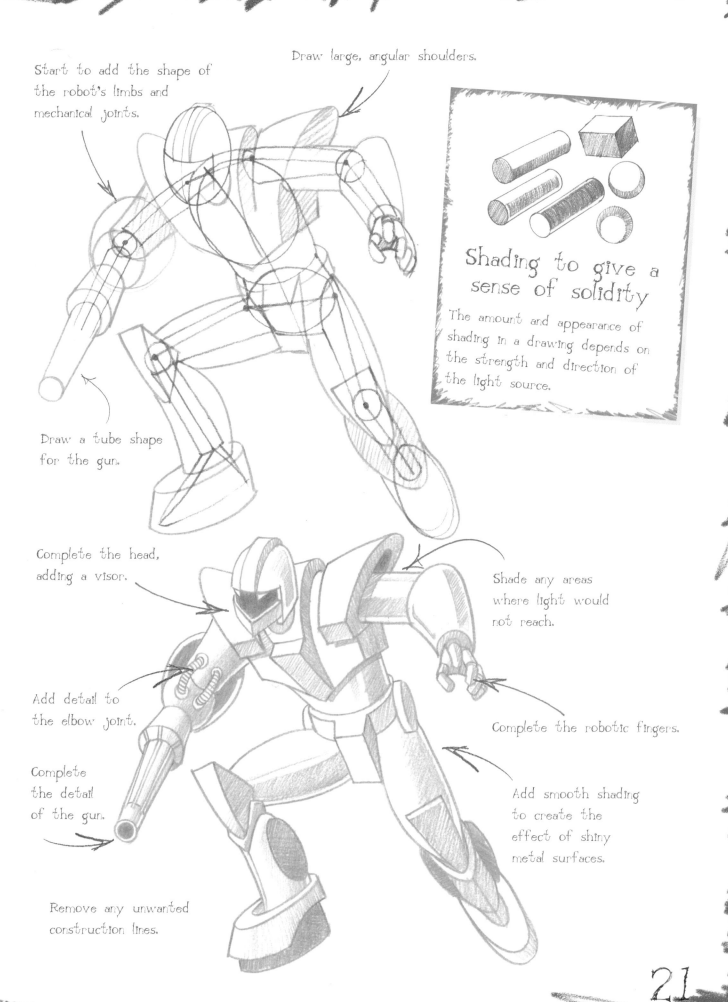

Draw large, angular shoulders.

Start to add the shape of the robot's limbs and mechanical joints.

Draw a tube shape for the gun.

Shading to give a sense of solidity

The amount and appearance of shading in a drawing depends on the strength and direction of the light source.

Complete the head, adding a visor.

Shade any areas where light would not reach.

Add detail to the elbow joint.

Complete the robotic fingers.

Complete the detail of the gun.

Add smooth shading to create the effect of shiny metal surfaces.

Remove any unwanted construction lines.

21

Action kick

This character is jumping in the air and doing a powerful high kick. The pose captures a sense of action and excitement.

Sketch in ovals for the head, body, hips, hands and feet.

Head

Body

Draw two lines to indicate the position and angle of the shoulders and hips.

Hips

Draw straight lines with dots at the joints for each of the limbs.

Fill out the arms and legs using simple tube shapes. The further arm looks small and the near leg very large because of the exaggerated perspective.

Indicate the position of the facial features.

Start to add the shape of the hands.

Add more detail to the shape of the feet.

Exaggerated features
Manga characters' facial features have a distinct style and shape. They often have oversized eyes which help when drawing expressions.

Add more detail to the facial features.

Draw in the shape of the fingers.

Finish drawing in the shape of the shoes.

Start drawing in the clothes. Make sure they curve around the body.

Draw in the clenched fist.

Draw straight lines coming from the kicking leg for added dramatic effect.

Finish drawing the detail of the hair and face.

Complete the detail of the clothing.

Add shading where light would not reach.

Add tone and creases to the clothing.

Remove any unwanted construction lines.

Defensive girl

This manga fighting girl is in a defensive pose, protecting her face, yet also ready to attack.

Draw in different sized ovals for the head, body, hands and hips.

Head

Body

Hips

Mark the positions of the eyes, nose and ear.

Draw in shapes for the clenched fists.

Draw limbs with straight lines.

Using the construction lines as a guide, start drawing in the main shapes of the body.

Indicate the joints with dots.

Draw in circles for the joints.

Draw in tube shapes for the legs.

Add more detail to the shape of the feet.

Sketch the flowing hair.

Add more detail to the face.

Draw in the fists.

Add the curved structure of the upper body and indicate the position of the belt.

Finish the detail of the hair using flowing lines.

Sketch the position of the trouser details.

Complete the face.

Add tone to the clothing by shading.

Finish the belt.

Draw in the details of the clothing.

Cropping an image

Choosing a small part of an image and adding a border and a dynamic background can give your drawing more impact. Try drawing straight lines coming out from the figure to create a dramatic effect!

Shade areas like this, where light wouldn't reach.

25

Falling in Fight

In battle it can be hard to keep your balance. This character is about to topple over and has a pained expression on his face.

Start by sketching these simple shapes for the figure.

Sketch an oval for the head.

Add an oval for the body and another for the hips.

Indicate the joints with dots.

Add fingers.

Draw two lines to indicate the position and angle of the shoulders and hips. Draw in a curved line for the spine (see page 12).

Sketch in the positions of the facial features.

Add circles for the joints.

Draw the limbs with straight lines.

Draw in the main shape of the body, using the ovals to guide you.

Draw triangle shapes to position the feet.

Using your construction lines as a guide, sketch the simple tube shapes for the arms and legs.

Add a flowing coat.

Add more detail to the face.

Shade areas like this, where light wouldn't reach.

Draw in the shape of the clothes, making sure that they curve around the body and flare out slightly at the ends of the limbs.

Finish the facial features and hair.

Add more detail to the boots.

Draw in movement lines to give a sense of action.

Add shading and tone to the clothes.

Complete the boots by shading and adding laces.

Remove any unwanted construction lines.

Using hair to add movement

Manga characters generally have very stylised hair. Hair can be affected by action or environment. For example, if the character is running, their hair may stream out behind them.

Fighting action!

These two manga figures are fighting. One of them is being thrown through the air by a swinging punch.

Draw ovals for the body, head and hips. Add straight lines for the limbs.

Head

Body

Hips

Draw dots for the joints.

Draw overlapping ovals for the body and hips.

Draw rounded shapes for the hands and feet.

Mark the position of the ear.

Draw simple tube shapes for the arms and legs.

Draw in the shapes of the body, using your construction lines as a guide.

Draw circles for joints.

Draw in the shape
of the hat.

Sketch in the fingers
and the outline of
the gloves.

Add more detail to
the facial features.

Draw the clothing around
the body and add shading.

Sketch in the
shoes and socks.

Add tone to
emphasise the muscles.

Finish off the
facial details.

Add shade to areas where
light would not reach.

Add movement
lines to create a
sense of action.

Complete the details
of the clothes.

Remove any unwanted
construction lines.

29

Vampire fight!

A manga hero is tackling a vicious vampire. The expressions on their faces should really show how they feel!

Start by sketching these simple shapes for the figures.

Sketch an oval for the head.

Draw the limbs with straight lines.

Sketch in the positions of the facial features.

Indicate the joints with dots.

Add circles for the joints.

Start sketching in the shape of the fingers and clenched fists.

Using your construction lines as a guide, sketch the simple tube shapes for the arms.

Add points to the vampire's ears.

Sketch a big turned-up collar and add shading.

Add spiky hair and start to finish the faces.

Start drawing the clothes.

Complete the hair using flowing lines.

Add fingers.

Sketch a large cuff onto the sleeve.

Finish off the facial detail and add fangs to the vampire.

Shade areas like this, where light wouldn't reach.

Finish all the detail of the clothing by adding shading and tone.

Complete the detail of the hands.

Carefully remove all construction lines.

Add the vampire's pointed claws.

31

Glossary

Construction lines Guidelines used in the early stages of a drawing which are usually erased later.

Cross-hatching A series of criss-crossing lines used to add shade to a drawing.

Fixative A type of resin used to spray over a finished drawing to prevent smudging. It should only be used by an adult.

Hatching A series of parallel lines used to add shade to a drawing.

Light source The direction from which the light seems to come in a drawing.

Pose The position assumed by a figure.

Profile A view from the side, especially a side view of a person's head or face.

Silhouette A drawing that shows only a dark shape, like a shadow.

Three-dimensional Having an effect of depth, so as to look lifelike or real.

Vanishing point The place in a perspective drawing where parallel lines appear to meet.

Index